THE NIGHT SKY
and Other
Amazing Sights in Space

Northern Lights

Nick Hunter

Heinemann
LIBRARY

Chicago, Illinois

To contact Capstone Global Library please
phone 800-747-4992, or visit our website
www.capstonepub.com

Edited by Rebecca Rissman, Daniel Nunn,
and Sian Smith
Designed by Joanna Hinton-Malivoire and Marcus Bell
Picture research by Mica Brancic
Production by Sophia Argyris
Originated by Capstone Global Library Ltd
Printed and bound in China by South China Printing
Company Ltd

17 16 15 14 13
10 9 8 7 6 5 4 3 2 1

Library of Congress Cataloging-in-Publication Data
Hunter, Nick.
  Northern lights / Nick Hunter.—1st ed.
      p. cm.—(The night sky: and other amazing sights)
Includes bibliographical references and index.
ISBN 978-1-4329-7516-6 (hb)
ISBN 978-1-4329-7521-0 (pb)

1. Auroras—Juvenile literature. 2. Solar wind—Juvenile
literature. 3. Magnetic fields—Juvenile literature. I. Title.
  QC971.4.H86 2014
  538'.768—dc23   2012043048

Acknowledgments
The author and publisher are grateful to the following
for permission to reproduce copyright material: Alamy
p.24 (© incamerastock/ICP); Capstone Publishers
pp.28, 29 (© Karon Dubke); Corbis p.25 (All Canada
Photos/© Robert Postma); Getty Images pp.20 (Chris
Wahlberg), 26 (Photolibrary/Chlaus Lotscher), 27
(Axiom Photographic Agency/Philip Lee Harvey); NASA
pp.9, 15 (Solar & Heliospheric Observatory), 16 (SOHO),
18 (NASA Scientific Visualization Studio Collection),
19 (JPL/Caltech), 21 (Courtesy 30th Space Wing,
Vandenberg Air Force Base), 23 (JPL/STScI (Space
Telescope Science Institute)); NOAA p.11; Science
Photo Library pp.12 (Detlev Van Ravenswaay), 17
(NASA), 22 (Walter Myers); Shutterstock pp.4 (© del.
Monaco), 5 (© Pi-Lens), 6 (© Roman Krochuk), 7 (©
Stephen Mcsweeny), 8 (© Leonello Calvetti), 10
(© Vitaly Korovin), 13 (© mexrix), 14 (© Triff).

Cover photograph of intense Aurora Borealis (Northern
Lights) reproduced with permission of Shutterstock (©
Pi-Lens).

We would like to thank Stuart Atkinson for his invaluable
help in the preparation of this book.

Contents

Some words are shown in bold, **like this**. You can find them in the glossary on page 30.

Out of This World

The night sky above us is full of lights. These lights are **stars** and **planets** far away in space. Most are bigger than planet Earth, where we live. They seem tiny because they are so far away.

You can see the night sky best in an area where there are no lights from streets or buildings.

4

This photograph of the Northern Lights was taken in Canada.

In some places on Earth, people see more than stars and planets in the sky. They see amazing lights called the Northern Lights.

What Are the Northern Lights?

The Northern Lights are the most exciting light show you could ever see. They can start with a pale green light in the sky.

Amazing lights like this only appear on some nights.

These campers have traveled to see the Northern Lights.

Sometimes, they become beautiful, bright sheets of light dancing across the night sky. The Northern Lights are called an **aurora**. Their full name is the aurora borealis.

Where Can You See the Northern Lights?

The Northern Lights are most often seen in places close to the North Pole. Sometimes people in Canada and Alaska can see the Northern Lights, too.

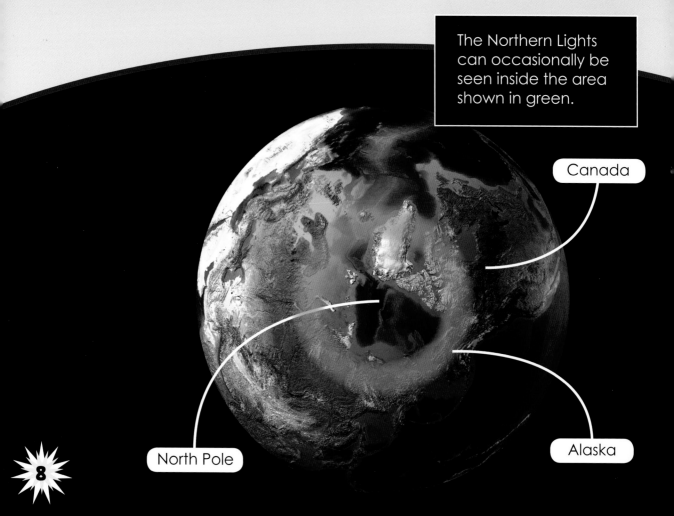

The Northern Lights can occasionally be seen inside the area shown in green.

Canada

Alaska

North Pole

8

Astronauts can see the Northern Lights from space.

The Northern Lights form high above the ground. They are usually around 60 miles (100 kilometers) up in Earth's **atmosphere**.

Southern Lights

There are also lights around the South Pole. The South Pole is on the frozen continent of Antarctica. This is one of the coldest places on Earth.

The land around the South Pole is always covered with ice.

This picture of the Southern Lights was taken in South Australia.

These lights are called the Southern Lights, or **aurora** australis. The Southern Lights can sometimes be seen in South America and Australia.

What Causes the Northern Lights?

The Northern Lights are caused by the Sun. The Sun is our nearest **star**. It sends out heat and light into space and to the **planets** in our **solar system**. Earth is just one of eight planets in our solar system.

Earth is the third planet from the Sun.

Sun

Earth

Energy from the Sun makes plants grow on Earth.

Without heat and light from the Sun, Earth would just be an icy rock in space. Plants, people, and other animals need **energy** from the Sun.

The Sun sends out a **solar wind**, as well as light and heat. The solar wind is an invisible stream of tiny **particles** of **energy**. These particles move across the **solar system** like a wind.

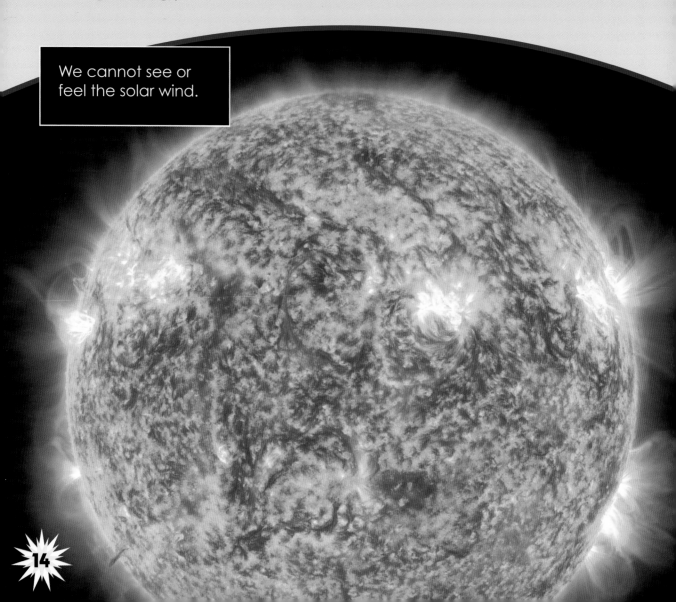

We cannot see or feel the solar wind.

The solar wind does not reach Earth's surface.

We can see the effects of the solar wind when it causes the Northern Lights. The light show is made by the solar wind hitting Earth's **atmosphere**.

Magnetic Earth

Earth is like a giant **magnet** with a **magnetic field** around it. Earth's magnetic field pushes the **particles** of the **solar wind** away from the **planet**.

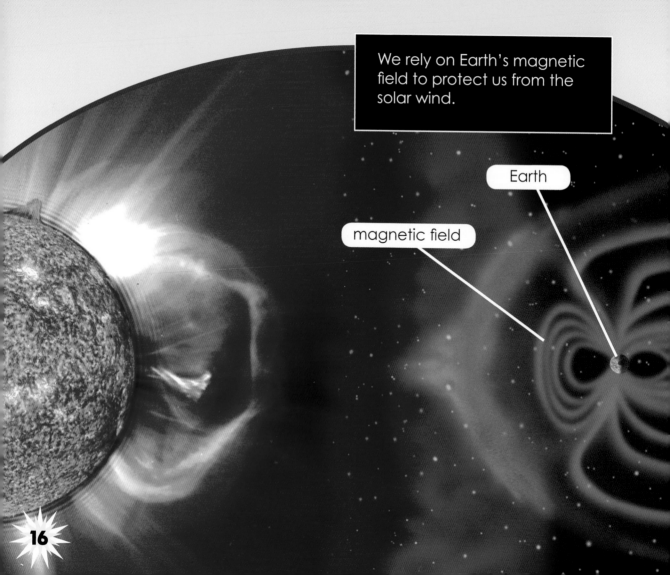

We rely on Earth's magnetic field to protect us from the solar wind.

Earth

magnetic field

This picture shows the South Pole, with the Southern Lights dancing around it.

The particles of the solar wind collect around the North and South Poles. That is why the Northern Lights can be seen near the North Pole, and Southern Lights can be seen near the South Pole.

Storms on the Sun

The **solar wind** is not always the same strength. Huge bursts of **energy** on the Sun's surface are called **solar flares**. These can cause solar storms, when the solar wind is much stronger.

A huge solar flare erupts from the Sun.

Many satellites are not protected from the solar wind by Earth's **magnetic field**.

One reason scientists study solar storms is that strong solar storms can damage satellites in space. Some televisions and special cell phones use satellites.

Studying the Sun

Astronomers study what is happening on the Sun. This tells them when the **solar wind** will be most powerful. Strong solar winds cause the Northern Lights.

Powerful **telescopes** are used to study the Sun, but you should never look at the Sun directly.

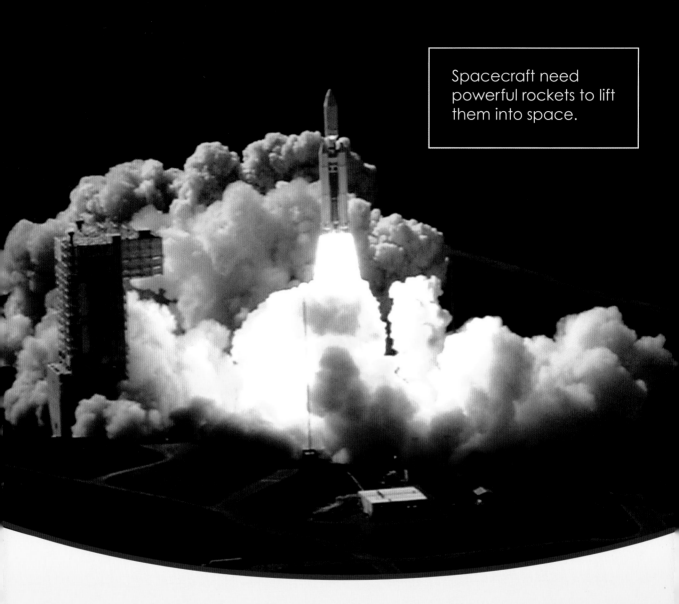

Spacecraft need powerful rockets to lift them into space.

Spacecraft can send back pictures and information to astronomers on Earth. This spacecraft is leaving to find out about the solar wind.

Across the Solar System

The **solar wind** also flows to **planets** far away from Earth. Jupiter is the biggest planet in our **solar system**.

Jupiter has its own northern and southern lights.

A **telescope** in space took this picture of auroras on Saturn.

Any planet with a **magnetic field** will have **auroras**. **Spacecraft** have sent back pictures of beautiful auroras around Saturn's poles.

Beliefs of the Past

People living near the North Pole had many beliefs about the Northern Lights. Some Inuit people still believe that you should never whistle at the lights. They may swoop down and carry you away.

Inuit people live in northern Canada, Alaska, and Greenland.

Ancient people did not know that the Northern Lights were caused by the **solar wind**.

When the Northern Lights are seen farther away from the North Pole, they often have a red color. In the past, people in Europe thought these red lights were a sign of war and bad times to come.

See for Yourself

To see the Northern Lights, you will have to visit a place where they can be seen. The farther north or south you go, the better your chances of seeing the **aurora**.

Luckily, you don't have to travel all the way to the North Pole to see the Northern Lights.

Many people travel to Norway, Alaska, Iceland, and Canada just to see the Northern Lights.

The Northern Lights can only be seen on a clear night or through gaps in the clouds. They are perfectly safe. They are many miles up in the sky.

Exploring Magnetic Fields

You don't need a whole **planet** to see how a **magnetic field** works.

What you need:

- a bar **magnet**
- a piece of paper
- iron filings.

What to do:

- Put the magnet on the paper. You could draw a planet, with the ends of the magnet as north and south poles.
- Drop some iron filings onto the paper.
- See the patterns the filings make around the magnet. This is the magnetic field.

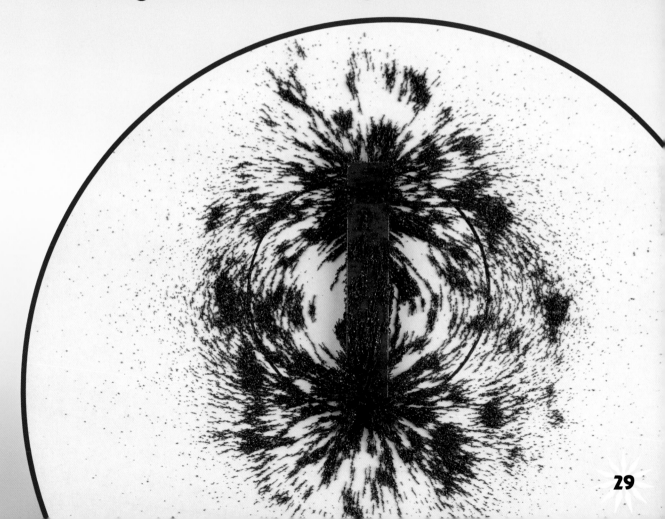

Glossary

astronaut person who travels into space in a spacecraft

astronomer person who studies space and the night sky

atmosphere layer of gases that surrounds a planet

aurora lights in the sky caused by the solar wind, such as the Northern and Southern Lights

energy power. Heat and light are forms of energy.

magnet something that creates a magnetic field and attracts or pushes away magnetic objects

magnetic field area where a magnet's force can be felt

particle tiniest possible piece of a material

planet large object (usually made of rock or gas) that orbits a star. Our planet, Earth, goes around the Sun.

solar flare large eruption or release of energy from the Sun's surface

solar system the Sun, eight planets, and many other small objects that travel around the Sun

solar wind stream of particles that flows from the Sun across the solar system

spacecraft object made by humans that travels into space

star huge ball of burning gas that produces massive amounts of heat and light

telescope device that astronomers use to make things in space look bigger

Find Out More

Books

Bingham, Caroline. *First Space Encyclopedia*. New York: DK Children, 2008.

Hunter, Nick. *The Sun* (Astronaut Travel Guides). Chicago: Raintree, 2012.

Trammel, Howard K. *The Solar System* (True Books: Space). Danbury, Conn.: Children's Press, 2009.

Underwood, Deborah. *Northern Lights*. San Diego: KidHaven, 2004.

Web sites

Facthound offers a safe, fun way to find Internet sites related to this book. All of the sites on Facthound have been researched by our staff.

Here's all you do:

Visit **www.facthound.com**

Type in this code: 9781432975166

Index

THE
Acorn's
Story

Some other Puffin picture books for you to enjoy:

JAFTA *and* JAFTA AND HIS MOTHER
Hugh Lewin/Lisa Kopper

KNOCK KNOCK, WHO'S THERE?
Sally Grindley/Anthony Browne

MOVING
Michael Rosen/Sophy Williams

NOT SO FAST SONGOLOLO
Niki Daly

OLIVER AND THE MONSTERS
Tony Blundell

THERE'S A BEAR IN THE BATH
Nanette Newman/Michael Foreman

THE THREE-LEGGED CAT
Margaret Mahy/Jonathan Allen

WINNI ALLFOURS
Babette Cole

THE
Acorn's
Story

Valerie Greeley

PUFFIN BOOKS

Who shook me free?
"*I*," said the breeze,
"*As I rustled the trees.*
I shook you free."

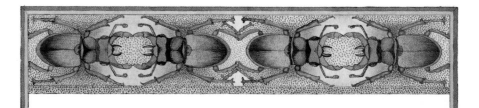

Who tilled the soil?
"We," said the pigs,
*"As we searched under twigs.
We tilled the soil."*

Who helped me root?
"I," said the rain,
"And it wasn't in vain.
I helped you root."

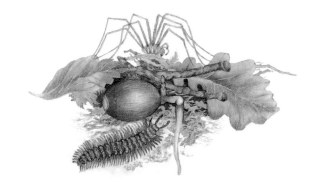

Who made me green?
"*I,*" said the light,
"*When the sun shone bright.
I made you green.*"

Who watched me grow?
"I," said the mouse,
"From my cosy house.
I watched you grow."

Who made me strong?
"I," said the earth,
"I broadened your girth.
I made you strong."

W ho made me change?
"*We,*" said the seasons,
"*We each had our reasons.*
We made you change."

W ho broke my bough?
"I," said the lightning,
"My power is frightening.
I broke your bough."

Who heard me cry?
"*I,*" said the owl,
"*As I watched the fox prowl.
I heard you cry.*"

Who'll tell my story?
"I," said your seed,
"For the whole world to read.
I'll tell your story."

PUFFIN BOOKS

Published by the Penguin Group
Penguin Books Ltd, 27 Wrights Lane, London W8 5TZ, England
Penguin Books USA Inc., 375 Hudson Street, New York, New York 10014, USA
Penguin Books Australia Ltd, Ringwood, Victoria, Australia
Penguin Books Canada Ltd, 10 Alcorn Avenue, Toronto, Ontario, Canada M4V 3B2
Penguin Books (NZ) Ltd, 182–190 Wairau Road, Auckland 10, New Zealand

Penguin Books Ltd, Registered Offices: Harmondsworth, Middlesex, England

First published by Blackie Children's Books 1994
Published in Puffin Books 1996
3 5 7 9 10 8 6 4 2

Made and printed in Italy by Printers srl – Trento